THE BOOK OF
CARDS FOR KIDS

by Gail MacColl
Illustrations by Simms Taback

WORKMAN PUBLISHING, NEW YORK

Library of Congress Cataloging-in-Publication Data
MacColl, Gail
The book of cards for kids/by Gail MacColl.
p.   cm.
Summary: Includes instructions and rules for over thirty card games, such as Go Fish,
Old Maid, Blackjack, and Klondike.
ISBN 1-56305-240-7
1. Card games–Juvenile literature.   2. Family recreation–Juvenile literature.
[1. Card games.   2. Games]   I. Title.
GV1244.M33 1992
795.4–dc20

Concept and design by Paul Hanson

Workman books are available at special discounts when purchased in bulk for premiums and sales promotions
as well as for fund-raising or educational use. Special editions or book excerpts can also be created to specification.
For details, contact the Special Sales Director at the address below.

Workman Publishing Company
708 Broadway
New York, NY 10003

Manufactured in the United States of America

First printing
10 9 8 7 6 5 4 3 2

CON-TENTS

CARDS FOR KIDS

THE • BIG DEAL

Playing Card History and Card Playing Basics

6

Playing cards and card games have been around for a long time. No one knows exactly where playing cards came  from; some people think it might have been the Middle East or Egypt. But the standard set, or deck, of cards— like your "Cards for Kids" deck— has existed for at least 500 years!

At first, playing cards were expensive to make. They were hand painted with gold and silver, and only very wealthy people could afford them. Naturally, the picture cards showed kings, queens, and knights dressed in the latest styles—of the year 1490, that is.

As more games were invented, the card decks changed. Cards were divided into groups called suits, and each suit had its own symbol. These symbols varied from one country to another, but eventually, when cards began to be printed instead of painted, four simple shapes were adopted:

♠ **SPADES**—a shovel symbol from German cards;

♣ **CLUBS**—from Spanish or German cards, which used sticks, oak leaves, or acorns as symbols;

♥ **HEARTS**—a shape used on German cards;

♦ **DIAMONDS**—invented by French card makers because it was an easy shape to print.

The printers made one more change in the deck. They decided to print hearts and diamonds in red, and clubs and spades in black.

About 150 years ago, one last big change was made in the look of playing cards. An English card maker put the number and suit

Old card   Squeezer

symbol along the edge of each card. These new cards were called "squeezers" because players could hold their cards squeezed together and still be able to tell what cards were in their hands.

Today, a standard deck of cards looks like the picture on the next page. The letter or number side of each card is called the face. The other side of all the cards has the same picture or pattern and is called the back.

Most decks include two Jokers, extra cards that are used in certain games and that come in handy as replacements for lost cards. A deck like this is familiar to people all over the world, so you can play card games wherever you travel. At different times and in different parts of the world, one game or another has become very popular. Whist, for instance, was the favorite English card game of the 19th century.

When many people play the same game, they often invent new forms of it. You may read that a game belongs to a certain family; that means it plays the same way, or is a version of that game. Out of the Whist family came Bridge, one of the most popular card games of the 20th century.

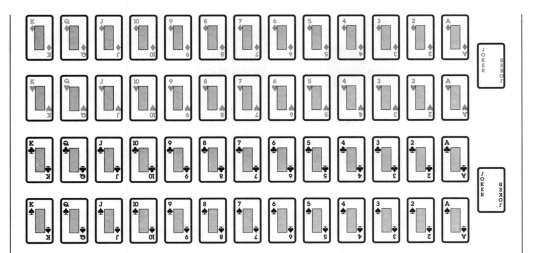

CARD SYMBOLS:

Card game instructions often use card symbols, to stand for specific cards. For instance, the Queen of Hearts would be written like this: Q♥. These symbols are printed on the card's edge.

PLAYING GAMES

When you play cards, you may use the cards in different ways. One game may have you match or collect cards with the same numbers or pictures, suits, or colors. Or you may gather cards that run in number order, which is called a sequence. In some games, you try to get rid of all your cards; in others, you try to collect as many cards as you can. Certain games ask you to remember what cards have already been played; other games ask you only to guess what card may be in another player's hand.

Most card players prefer to sit around a table so that everyone can see the cards being played. Or you can sit on the floor in a circle; as long as the cards in the center can be seen and the cards in the other players' hands cannot be seen!

Almost all card games have the same rules for starting a game, for handling the cards, and for card manners:

SHUFFLE

Most games are started by mixing the cards together so well that their order is unpredictable. Some card players have learned fancy shuffling, but any kind of card mixing will work, as long as all cards have the pattern (or back) side facing up when you're finished. Always shuffle at least five times before beginning a new game.

DEAL

At the beginning of most games, one person hands out, or deals, the cards to each player. The dealer can be chosen by picking the highest cards, or simply by asking the oldest or youngest player to deal. The best way to deal cards is to hold the deck, face down, in one hand and to slide off the top card with the thumb and forefinger of the other hand, placing the card face down on the table in front of the other player. Always deal out cards one at a time and face down, starting with the player on your left.

CUT

Players used to cut cards to make sure the dealer wasn't cheating. Today they do it because it's just good card manners. To cut the deck, the player to the left of the dealer

lifts about half the cards off the top of a face-down deck and puts them beside the bottom half. Then the dealer picks up the bottom half, puts it on the top half, picks up the entire deck, and deals. You can also cut cards as a way to choose a dealer. Each player lifts up a portion of the deck and shows the bottom card. The player who revealed the highest card is the dealer.

SECRECY

Most of the fun of card games is not knowing what cards the other players are holding, or what card may turn up next in the deck. If you try too hard to look at other players' cards—by peeking, or by having a friend signal to you, or in many other ways people have invented over the years— you're not really playing the game. That's why players learn to play their cards "close to the vest" (not letting anyone else see them), and why they put on a "poker face" (not letting their expression tell players whether they have winning or losing cards). If you become skilled at playing cards, you're likely to win anyway. And if you play a game with no skill involved, then it's just "the luck of the draw" (you win if you happen to pick the right card at the right time).

KEEPING SCORE

Many card games use point scoring to determine the winner. To play these games you'll need to keep a score sheet and record the points won by each player. A plain sheet of paper marked as shown will start your score sheet. Write in the points according to game instructions.

The games in this book begin with the easiest and move to the more difficult. If you find a word you don't know, look it up in Card Words on page 137.

CARDS FOR KIDS

SNAP

2–4 PLAYERS

A great game for beginners. Loud, lively, and easy.

OBJECT OF THE GAME
To win all the cards.

SET UP

ALL PLAYERS: Pick a card from the deck. Whoever has the highest card is the dealer.

START

DEALER: Shuffle the cards.

Deal them all out, face down and one at a time. It doesn't matter if some players have more cards than others.

ALL PLAYERS: Put all your cards, face down, in a stack in front of you.

PLAY

PLAYER ON DEALER'S LEFT: You go first. Take the top card from your stack, turn it over, and place it face up beside your stack.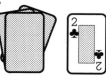

NEXT PLAYER: Do the same. Watch for two face-up cards with matching numbers or letters.

• Play goes around to the left, with each player turning up a card. If you run out of cards, turn over your face-up pile and use it again.

• Keep an eagle eye out for the moment when two matching cards appear. Immediately shout "Snap!" Gather up the two piles with  the matching cards and add them to the bottom of your own face-down stack.

15

• If you shout "Snap!" by mistake, you must give each of the other players a card from your face-down stack.

● If two of you shout "Snap!" at exactly the same time, put the piles with the matching cards in the center. This is the "snap pool." If you turn up a card that matches the snap pool card, you add the cards in the snap pool to the bottom of your face-down stack.

● When you run out of cards, you're out of the game. The winner is the player who ends up with all the cards.

WINNER: Gather up the cards, shuffle them, and deal the next game.

VARIATIONS

BABY SNAP: There are two players and only one face-up pile in the center. You take turns turning up cards from your face-down stacks. When you see matching cards, shout "Snap!" and add the face-up cards to your stack.

SPEED SNAP: Everyone turns up cards at the same time instead of taking turns. Very fast-moving and noisy.

CARDS FOR KIDS

•OLD•
MAID

3–6 PLAYERS

An oldie but a goody. Also called Pass the Lady. Easy to learn, fun, and short.

OBJECT OF THE GAME

Players get rid of all their cards by making pairs. The player left with the Queen of Spades is the Old Maid.

SET UP

● Find the four Queens in the deck of cards. Take out the Queen of Spades and put it back in the deck.

● Set the other three Queens to one side — you won't be needing them for this game. Shuffle the cards.

START

DEALER: Deal out all the cards, one at a time, face down. It's all right if some players have more cards than others.

ALL PLAYERS: Look at your cards — without letting anyone else see what you have. Any pairs you find go back on the table, face down. If you have three cards with the same number, one stays in your hand. If you have four cards — 2 pairs — all four can go down.

PLAY

PLAYER ON DEALER'S LEFT: You go first. Make a fan of your cards and show them, *face down,* to the player on your left.

NEXT PLAYER: Pick a card from the fan. If the card makes a pair with one you already have, put the new pair face down on the table. If not, the card goes into your hand. Now fan out your cards for the player sitting to your left, for her to choose from.

● Play goes around in a circle, with players choosing cards

and putting down pairs, until everyone has run out of cards. Everyone, that is, except the person holding the Old Maid — the Queen of Spades.

ALL PLAYERS: Everyone shouts "Old Maid!" and the game is over. The Old Maid picks up the cards and deals the next round.

LE VIEUX GARÇON: In this French version, three Jacks are removed, leaving the J♠, or the "old boy," in the deck.

LE POUILLEUX: Remove the J♣ from the deck. Pairs must match for color and number. The player left holding the odd Jack is the "lice man."

19

• GO • FISH

3–6 PLAYERS

A classic. Even very young children can win this game without help from grownups. But it's lively enough for everyone in the family.

20

OBJECT OF THE GAME

To get rid of all your cards by collecting books. Four matching cards make a book.

SET UP

ALL PLAYERS: Pick a card from the deck. The player with the highest card deals the first round.

START

DEALER: Shuffle the cards. Deal them out, face down and one at a time. If you have three players, deal out seven cards to each. If you have four or more players, each player gets five cards.

●Spread the rest of the cards face down in the center. This is the fishing pile.

ALL PLAYERS: Pick up your cards. Hold them very carefully so that no one else can see them. Arrange the cards so that the ones that match—two

Sixes, for example, or three Queens—are next to each other.

PLAYER ON DEALER'S LEFT: You go first. Look at your hand and decide what cards you need to make a book. Then ask any other player whether he has any of the cards you want. For instance, you might ask, "Do you have any Sixes?" If the player has any Sixes, he gives them to you. You may then ask any player for another card you need.

●You can keep asking for cards and making books as long as the other players have what you are looking for.

OTHER PLAYERS: If you don't

21

have any of the cards the first player wants, say "Go fish." That player then picks a card from the fish pile and puts it in his hand. His turn is over.

Remember: There are only four cards of every number and picture! Put the completed book in a stack, face down, in front of you.

● Play goes around to the left, with each player asking and fishing and putting down books.

● The first person to get rid of all his or her cards wins. If two players run out of cards at the same time, the one with the most books is the winner.

PLAYER ON DEALER'S LEFT:
Gather up the cards. You are the dealer for the next game.

VARIATIONS

LITTLE FISH: Simpler version for very young children. Deal out all cards—there is no stack in the middle. Collect pairs instead of books. The winner is the player with the most pairs.

BIG FISH: Make the game a little harder by having to ask

STRATEGY

Listen to what other players are asking for, even if it's not your turn. If you can remember who was asking for Sevens a minute or two ago, that's who you'll ask to give you Sevens when it's your turn.

Keep in mind that a player's hand changes every time she picks a card from the fish pile. It's possible that someone who had no Sixes the last time you asked has one now.

for the number and suit of the card you want. For instance, "Do you have the Six of Hearts?" rather than "Do you have any Sixes?"

SLAP-JACK

3–5 PLAYERS

Easy and action-packed. A favorite for families with young children.

OBJECT OF THE GAME

To win all the cards. To be fair, cards should be turned up facing away from the player, so everyone has the same chance to spot the Jacks.

SET UP

ALL PLAYERS: Pick a card from the deck. Whoever has

the highest card is the dealer for the first round.

DEALER: Shuffle the cards. Deal them all out, face down and one at a time. Some players may have more cards than others.

ALL PLAYERS: Do not look at your cards. Put them in a face-down stack in front of you.

PLAYER ON DEALER'S LEFT: You go first. Take the top card off your stack and put it face up in the center.

NEXT PLAYER: Do the same, placing your card on top of the card just played.

● Play goes around the circle until someone plays a Jack. As

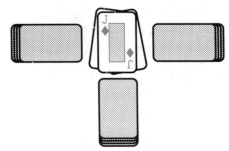

soon as you see the Jack on the pile, slap your hand down on top of it.

● If you're the first to slap the Jack, take the whole pile from the center and mix it in with your own stack.

● The player to your left will

25

start off the next round by playing a card from the top of her stack.

ALL PLAYERS: If you run out of cards, you have one last chance to stay in the game.

●Try to be the first person to slap the next Jack. Then you can take the pile and play on. Otherwise, you drop out of the game.

●If you slap a card that isn't a Jack, you must give a card to each of the other players. The game is over when one player wins all the cards.

WINNER: Shuffle the cards—you are the dealer for the next game.

VARIATION

●To keep things short and sweet, use a timer. Decide ahead of time how long the game will be—maybe five or ten minutes. Then set the timer—the person with the most cards when the timer sounds is the winner.

ANIMAL NOISES

2–6 PLAYERS

A truly noisy card game. It's better known in a version called Menagerie or Animals—but this is the really fun game.

OBJECT OF THE GAME

To win all the cards.

SET UP

ALL PLAYERS: Decide what animal you want to be. Make that animal's noise—meow, squeak, quack, whatever. Each player should choose a different animal.

27

● Make sure the other players know what animal you're supposed to be. And remember what animals they are, too— you'll need to know.

● Everyone picks a card from the deck. Whoever has the highest card deals.

START

DEALER: Shuffle the cards. Deal them all out one at a time and face down. It doesn't matter if some people have more cards than others.

ALL PLAYERS: Do *not* look at your cards. Put them in a face-down stack in front of you.

PLAY

PLAYER ON DEALER'S LEFT: You go first. Turn over the top card and put it beside your stack, face up so everyone can see it.

● Everyone takes a turn, with play going around to the left. Each player turns up a card.

● Keep an eye out for the moment when someone else turns up a card that matches— by number or picture—your face-up card. You may have a few turns before this happens.

● As soon as you spot the

match, make the other player's animal noise three times in a row. Then take the other player's face-up pile and add it to your face-down stack.

● If both players spot the match at the same time, the first one to finish making the noises gets the pile.

● If you make the wrong noise, you have to give your face-up pile to the player with the matching card.

●If you run out of cards in your face-down stack, just turn over your face-up pile and keep going.

● The game ends when one person has won all the cards.

WINNER: Gather up the cards and deal the next game.

VARIATION

MENAGERIE: Everyone thinks of animals with long names, such as duck-billed platypus, orangutan, or hippopotamus. Write the names on pieces of paper and mix them together in a bowl or hat. Each player picks a name from the hat; that's his or her animal for the game. Let all the other players know which animal you are. When you spot a matching card, you must shout three times the name of the other player's animal.

• MY • SHIP SAILS

4–7 PLAYERS

The more the merrier. This game is easy enough for beginners, but it's at its best when played at a rapid-fire pace.

OBJECT OF THE GAME

To be the first player to collect seven cards of the same suit.

SET UP

ALL PLAYERS: Pick a card from the deck. Whoever has the highest card deals the first round.

START

DEALER: Shuffle the cards. Deal out seven cards to each player, one at a time and face down.

● Put the rest of the deck to one side—you won't be using it again for this game.

ALL PLAYERS: Pick up your cards. Arrange them into suits so that you can easily see what you have most of.

● Decide what suit to collect. But be prepared to change your mind during the game.

● Choose a card that you don't want. Put that card face down in front of you.

ALL PLAYERS: Slide the card you don't want to your left-hand neighbor. Pick up the card your right-hand neighbor slides to you.

● Keep on passing and picking up cards, trying to get a hand of cards all of the same suit.

● The first person to have seven cards of the same suit shouts "My Ship Sails!" and is the winner.

AUTHORS

4–6 PLAYERS

This game used to be played with cards that showed authors and the titles of their books. The same game goes by the name Happy Families.

32

OBJECT OF THE GAME

To collect as many books as possible. A book is all four cards of the same number or letter, one from each suit.

SET UP

ALL PLAYERS: Pick a card from the deck. The player with the highest card deals.

START

DEALER: Shuffle the cards. Deal out all the cards, one at a time and face down. It's all right if some players have more cards than others.

ALL PLAYERS: Look at your cards. Arrange them so that cards with the same number are side by side in your hand.

PLAY

PLAYER ON DEALER'S LEFT:
You go first. Decide what cards you need to make a book. Ask one of the other players for one of those cards. You must ask for the exact card—for instance, the 9♠.

ALL PLAYERS: If you are asked for a card and you have it, you must hand it over. But if you only have a similiar card—for instance, the 9♣—say, "No."

Warning: If you say you don't have a card when you do, you'll pay a penalty when the other players find out—you'll have to give one of your cards to each of the other players.

● Play goes around to the left, with each player asking for cards and collecting books.

● When you have a book of four matching cards, show it to the other players, then put it face down in front of you.

● If you run out of cards by

making a book, you must sit out the rest of  the game. You will still count up the number of books you collected for scoring at the end of the game.

● When all the books have been collected and everyone is out of cards the game is over. The player with the most books is the winner.

PLAYER ON DEALER'S LEFT:
When everyone has finished counting their books, gather

EMILY BRONTE

up the cards. You will deal the next game.

34

•WAR•

2 PLAYERS

For the serious player, this game can be a real test of stamina and will.

OBJECT OF THE GAME

To win all the cards.

SET UP

BOTH PLAYERS: Pick a card from the deck. The player with the highest card deals.

START

DEALER: Shuffle the cards. Deal them all out, one at a time and face down.

BOTH PLAYERS: Place your cards face down in a stack in front of you. Do not look at them.

PLAY

• At the same time, each of you turns over her top card and puts it in the center so that the two cards are side by side. Whoever has the higher card takes both cards and adds them, face down, to the bottom of her stack.

BOTH PLAYERS: Play goes on in the same way until both players turn over a card of the same rank—two Kings, for example. This is War.

• Each player puts one card face down, then another card face up, on top of his turned-up card. The higher face-up card wins all six cards.

• If the top cards match again, repeat the War.

• The player who collects all the cards is the winner.

WINNER: Shuffle the cards and deal the next game.

VARIATIONS

● Set a time limit. The winner is the person who has the most cards when the time is up.

DOUBLE WAR: For three players. Deal out all the cards except for the last one, so that everyone has seventeen cards. When any two cards of the same rank are turned up, all three players are at War. When all three players turn up matching cards, you're at Double War. Everyone must put two cards face down before putting out the face-up card. If two cards match again,

return to single War.

PERSIAN PASHA. Instead of putting the turned-up cards in the middle, each of you puts them next to your face-down stack. When two turned-up cards are of the same suit, the higher ranking card wins, and that player takes the other player's entire face-up pile to add to his own face-down stack.

CONCEN-TRATION

2–4 PLAYERS

A test of observation, the game is also known as Memory or as Pelmanism.

OBJECT OF THE GAME

To collect as many cards as possible by making pairs.

SET UP

● Use a large flat area, such as a big table or the floor. Shuffle the cards well.

● Lay the cards out, face down, in a large rectangle. Make sure the cards do not touch each other.

● Decide who will go first; the youngest, perhaps, or by alphabetical order of first names.

START

FIRST PLAYER: Turn over any two cards, being careful not to disturb the nearby cards.

If the turned-over cards are the same number or letter—two Sixes, for instance—pick them up and put them beside you. Then turn over two more cards.

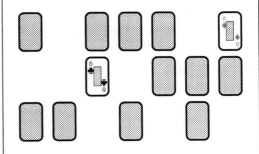

● If the cards don't match, turn them back over in the same position they were in. Your turn is finished.

PLAY

NEXT PLAYER: Turn over another card. If it matches the number or letter of a card you've already seen, try to remember where you saw that one and turn it over.

● If you make a match, pick up the two cards and put them beside you. If not, turn the cards back over.

● Players take turns, turning over cards and trying to make pairs. A turn lasts as long as a player can make pairs.

● When all the cards have been picked up, the game is over. The player with the most pairs is the winner.

WINNER: Gather up the cards, shuffle them, and lay them out for another game.

VARIATIONS

● Pairs must be of the same rank *and* color—two red Sixes, for instance.

● To make an easier, faster game, remove the Twos, Threes, Fours, Fives, and Sixes from the deck.

STRATEGY

Watch closely when other players are turning over cards. Don't lose interest just because it isn't your turn.

DON-KEY

4–6 PLAYERS

A fast-moving, noisy game for the whole family.

OBJECT OF THE GAME

Don't be a donkey! For each round you lose, you get a letter. Six lost rounds spells D-O-N-K-E-Y.

41

SET UP

• From the regular deck, pull out a book of four matching cards, one book for each player. For instance, for four play-

ers, pull out all the Aces, Kings, Queens, and Jacks.

● Put the rest of the deck to one side—you won't be needing it again for this game. Shuffle these books together.

● Collect some nonbreakable objects—spoons, for example. You'll need one spoon fewer than the number of players. (Three spoons for four players, and so on.) Put the spoons in the middle of a table.

● Write each player's name on a sheet of paper, leaving plenty of room either next to or underneath each name.

● Everyone picks a card from the deck. Whoever has the highest card deals the first round.

START

DEALER: Deal out the cards, face down and one at a time, to each player. Each player should have four cards.

ALL PLAYERS: Pick up your cards. Don't let anyone else see them. Choose a card you don't want and slide it, face down on the table, to the person sitting on your left.

PLAY

ALL PLAYERS: Pick up the card you've been passed. Either put it with the rest of your cards or slide it along again. You are trying to collect a book—four Kings, for instance.

● When you collect a book of four matching cards, quietly put it face down on the table and pick up one of the spoons.

ALL PLAYERS: As soon as you see someone pick up a spoon, put down your cards and try to pick up a spoon yourself.

● The player left without a spoon loses the round and gets a "D" written beside his name on the score sheet. The next time that player loses he gets an "O," and so on.

LOSER: Collect the cards — except the ones you put aside — shuffle them and deal the next round.

● The first player to have "D-O-N-K-E-Y" written out beside his name is the loser, and must say "Hee-haw!"

VARIATION

PIG: The first person to collect a book puts his finger beside his nose. Everyone else does the same. The last person to put his finger to his nose is the pig, and must say "Oink, oink."

· GO · BOOM

2–6 PLAYERS

44

Although this game requires almost no skill and everyone can play, it's also a first lesson in taking tricks.

OBJECT OF THE GAME

To get rid of all your cards. Try to avoid having to pick cards from the center stack.

SET UP

ALL PLAYERS: Pick a card from the deck. The player whose card is highest deals the first round.

START

DEALER: Shuffle the cards. Deal out seven cards, one at a time and face down, to each player. Put the rest of the cards, face down, in the center.

ALL PLAYERS: Pick up your cards and arrange them from the highest (Aces) on the left to the lowest (Twos) on the right.

PLAY

PLAYER TO DEALER'S LEFT: You go first. Put a card from your hand face up in the center.

NEXT PLAYER: Choose a card from your hand that is the same number or from the same suit as the card just played. Put it face up in the center.

● If you can't match the face-up card, start picking cards from the face-down stack in the center until you find a card that does match, either by suit or by number. Put it face up in the center.

● If there are more than four players, pick from the face-down stack only three times. If you haven't made a match after the third try, say "Pass."

- Play goes around in a circle, with each player trying to match the first card. After each player has had a turn, the round is finished.

- The dealer clears away the cards in the face-up pile after each round.

- The player who played the highest card in the round starts off the next round. If there is a tie for highest card, whoever played it first starts off.

- When the face-down pile in the center runs out, players who can't match from their hands say "Pass."

- The first player to get rid of all his cards shouts "Boom!" and is the winner.

PLAYER ON DEALER'S LEFT: Gather up the cards. You will deal the next game.

VARIATION

SCORING GO BOOM: Decide ahead of time what the winning number of points will be—usually about 200. When you go "Boom!" all the other players give you the cards left in their hands. For every face card (King, Queen, or Jack), you get 10 points. For the number cards, you get "face value"—that means the number on the card is the number

STRATEGY

Watch carefully what cards the other players are putting down. Then you can work out what cards you want to keep (if you have a choice) for later on. For instance, if someone is playing a lot of high cards, hold on to your low cards; they're bound to start showing up later. If a lot of red cards are being played, keep your clubs and spades.

of points you score. Aces are worth 1 point. The first player to score 200 points wins.

BEGGAR
• YOUR •
NEIGHBOR

2–4 PLAYERS

An ancient
game full
of changing
fortunes.
A favorite with
Lady Luck.

OBJECT OF THE GAME

To win all the cards.

SET UP

ALL PLAYERS: Pick a card from the deck. The player with the highest card deals.

START

DEALER: Shuffle the cards. Deal them all out, one at a time and face down. It's okay if some players have more cards than others.

ALL PLAYERS: Do not look at your cards. Put them in a face-down stack in front of you.

PLAY

PLAYER ON DEALER'S LEFT: You go first. Take the top card from your stack and put it face up in the center.

ALL PLAYERS: Take turns going around the table to the left, turning up cards and putting them in the center.

● If you turn up a face card (a King, Queen, or Jack) or an

Ace, stop. Demand payment from the player sitting on your left as follows:

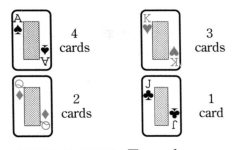

A♠ 4 cards
K♥ 3 cards
Q♦ 2 cards
J♣ 1 card

49

NEXT PLAYER: To make payment, you must turn up the cards, one at a time, from your face-down stack and add them to the pile in the center.

● If you turn up a face card or an Ace, stop. Demand payment, according to the card you turned up, from the player sitting on your left. Your neighbor must now pay; if she turns up a face card, she demands payment from her neighbor on the left, and so on.

● When one of you fails to turn up an Ace or a face card as payment, the pile in the center goes to whoever turned up the last Ace or face card. That player adds it to the bottom of his face-down stack, and starts a new round by playing the top card from his stack.

● When you lose all your cards, you are out of the game. The player who collects all the cards is the winner.

WINNER: Shuffle the cards and deal the next game.

VARIATIONS

● Set a time limit. The person with the most cards when time runs out is the winner. Or, remove the Twos, Threes, Fours, and Fives from the deck. If that makes the game too quick, put the Fives back in.

● For a two-handed version, each of you takes half the deck. When a face card or an Ace appears, demand payment. If your opponent turns up a face card, you must make payment. If he does not turn up a face card, you get the center pile.

•PLAY•
OR PAY

3–7 PLAYERS

A sequence game (cards are played in number order) also known as Round the Corner.

OBJECT OF THE GAME

To win as many counters as possible in each round. Aces are both high and low.

51

SET UP

• Decide how many rounds the game will be —ten is a good number to start with. Each deal is a round.

● Find some counters. You can use paper clips, pennies, small blocks, or M&Ms. Give 20 counters to each player.

ALL PLAYERS: Pick a card from the deck. Whoever has the highest card deals the first round.

START

DEALER: Shuffle the cards. Deal them all out face down and one at a time. It's okay if some players have more cards than others.

ALL PLAYERS: Pick up your cards. Don't let anyone else see what you have. Arrange your hand by suit and number—put all the cards from one suit together, with the highest card in each suit on the left.

PLAY

PLAYER ON DEALER'S LEFT: You go first. Choose one card from a suit you have a lot of, and put it down in the center.

NEXT PLAYER: Do you have the next highest card in the sequence (in number order)? For instance, if the first player has put down the 3♦, you'll have to put down the 4♦.

- If you can play in number order, put your card on top of the first card.

- If you can't, you must put one counter into the center.

- Play goes around to the left, with each player putting down a card in number order, or putting out a counter.

- When an Ace is played on a King, you go "round the corner" and continue the sequence with the Two.

- If you have played the last card in a suit, start another sequence by playing any card you like from your hand.

- The first person to play all of her cards wins the round and takes all the counters from the middle.

LOSERS: You must each give the winner one counter for every card still left in your hand.

PLAYER ON DEALER'S LEFT: Gather up the cards, shuffle them well, and deal the next round.

- The person with the most counters after the agreed-upon number of rounds is the winner of the game.

• SNIP •
SNAP
SNOREM

5–6 PLAYERS

An old, much-loved game with lots of action. Appeals especially to chatterboxes.

54

OBJECT OF THE GAME

To get rid of all your cards by matching rank.

SET UP

ALL PLAYERS: Pick a card from the deck. The player with the highest card is the dealer.

START

DEALER: Shuffle the cards. Deal them all out, one at a time and face down. It's all right if some players have more cards than others.

ALL PLAYERS: Arrange your cards in order of rank from the highest (Aces) on the left to the lowest (Twos) on the right.

PLAY

PLAYER ON DEALER'S LEFT: You go first. Choose one card and put it face up in the center.

NEXT PLAYER: If you have a card that matches (is the same number), put

it down next to the first card and shout "Snip!" If you have two cards that match, save the other for your next turn. If you don't have a matching card, say "Pass."

● Play goes around to the left, with each player matching or passing.

● If you play the second matching card, shout "Snap!"

● If you play the third matching card, shout "Snorem!" You then start the next round by putting a new card into the center.

● The first player to get rid of all his cards is the winner.

● To make the game faster, put down all your matching cards in one turn, shouting "Snip, snap!" or "Snip, snap, snorem!"

JIG: Instead of matching rank, put down cards in sequence (number order). For example, if there is a Five in the center, put a Six, then a Seven, then an Eight on it, not necessarily of the same suit. Shout "Jiggety, joggety, jig" instead of "Snip, snap snorem." For added difficulty, follow the sequence and the suit.

EARL OF COVENTRY: Instead of saying "Snip, snap, snorem" when putting out cards, you speak in a series of rhymes. The player putting the first card into the center (an Eight for instance), says: "There's as good as Eight can be." The next player to match says "There's an Eight as good as he." The third player to put out an Eight says "There's the best of all the three," and the last player puts out the final Eight and says "And there's the Earl of Coventry!"

GIVE AWAY

2–6 PLAYERS

Easy and fast. The trick here is to keep your eye on two or more piles at the same time.

OBJECT OF THE GAME

To be the first to get rid of all your cards by playing them in sequence (number order).

SET UP

ALL PLAYERS: Pick a card from the deck. Whoever has the highest card deals the first game.

START

DEALER: Shuffle the deck. Deal out all the cards, one at a time and face down. It's okay if some players have more cards than others.

ALL PLAYERS: Put your cards in a face-down stack in front of you. Do not look at them.

PLAY

PLAYER ON DEALER'S LEFT: You go first. Turn over your top card. If it is an Ace, put it in the middle and turn over another card. If it is not an Ace, put it face up beside your stack.

NEXT PLAYER: Turn over your top card. If it is a Two of the same suit as the Ace already played, put it on top of the Ace in the middle and turn over another card.

● But if it follows in number order, either up or down, the first player's face-up card (it

doesn't need to be the same suit), put it on top of the other player's card and turn over another card from your stack.

● If you can't play the

card, end your turn by starting your own face-up pile.

● Play goes around to the left, with players turning up cards and playing them in number order, either to the center or to other players' face-up piles.

● A turn lasts as long as you can play a card from your face-down stack to a center pile or to another player's face-up pile.

● You can also play cards from your own face-up pile.

● You must play a card onto a center pile if possible.

● If you run out of face-down cards while it's still your turn,

immediately turn over your own face-up pile and keep playing. If your last card is played onto your own face-up pile, wait until your next turn before turning over the pile.

● The first player to get rid of all her cards by playing them into the center or onto other face-up piles is the winner.

59

STRATEGY

Play your card onto the face-up pile of the player with the fewest cards, to keep him from winning.

STEALING BUNDLES

2 PLAYERS

Another good game for matching rank, this one belongs to the Casino family of card games. Also known as Old Man's Bundle and Stealing the Old Man's Bundle.

60

OBJECT OF THE GAME

To collect the most cards.

SET UP

BOTH PLAYERS: Pick a card from the deck. The player with the highest card deals.

DEALER: Shuffle the cards. Deal four cards to yourself, face down, and four cards to your opponent, face down. Deal four more cards face up on the table between you. Put the rest of the deck to one side for the moment.

OPPONENT: You go first. Do you have a card that matches in rank one of the cards in the center?

● If so, "capture" the card in the center with the matching card from your hand and put it in a face-up pile beside you. This is your "bundle."

● If you have no matching cards you must "trail"—put a card from your hand face up in the middle.

DEALER: If you have a card that matches one in the center, capture it. If you have a card that matches the face-up card on your opponent's bundle, "steal" the bundle and add it to your own face-up pile.

61

• You must add cards to your face-up pile in the exact order in which they were captured. In any one turn you can capture as many cards from the center as you have matching cards in your hand.

EACH PLAYER: Keep taking turns trying to match cards, add to your bundle, and steal the other player's bundle.

DEALER: When both of you have played all four cards from your hand, use the stack you put aside at the start to deal four more cards to each of you. Do not deal any more cards to the center.

• When all cards have been dealt and played the game is over. Whoever captured the last match from the center takes any other cards left there.

• The player with the most cards in his bundle wins.

WINNER: Gather up the cards, shuffle them, and deal the next round.

CHASE • THE • ACE

5 OR MORE PLAYERS

A game of three lives, and three chances to win. Also called Ranter-Go-Round and Cuckoo.

OBJECT OF THE GAME

To win the pool by not being left with the lowest card. Kings are high and Aces are low in this game.

SET UP

63

You will need three counters for each player. Use pennies, paper clips, building blocks, or cookies.

ALL PLAYERS: Pick a card from the deck. The player with the highest card is the dealer for the first round.

DEALER: Give every player three counters. Each counter represents a "life." Shuffle the deck and deal each player one card, face down.

PLAY

PLAYER ON DEALER'S LEFT: Look at your card. If it is a high card you'll want to keep it. Say "Stand."

● If it is a low card you'll want to get rid of it. Slide the card, face down, to your left-hand neighbor and say "Change!"

LEFT-HAND NEIGHBOR: You must change cards with the player when ordered to do so, unless the card you are holding is a King. If so, you say "King!" and show your King; the player then asks the person on your left.

● If the card you receive is an Ace, Two, or Three, you must tell the other players. Because it is the lowest card, the Ace will keep moving around the circle.

● If you do change cards, it is your turn to decide whether to stand or change with the player on your left. Play continues around to the left until it is the dealer's turn.

DEALER: You are last in the round, so you can't ask to change cards with anyone. If you don't like the card you are holding, bury it in the middle of the deck and pick another card from the top. Show the card to the other players.

● If it is a King, you automatically lose the hand and a life. Put one counter in the "pool" (a pile of counters that will go to the winner).

ALL PLAYERS: When the dealer shows you his card, turn up yours. Whoever has the lowest card loses a life and must put a counter in the pool.

● If there is a tie for lowest card, each player in the tie puts a counter in the pool.

PLAYER ON DEALER'S LEFT: Gather up all the cards and put them at the bottom of the deck. Deal the next round.

● When you lose all three of your lives, you are out of the game.

● The last player to have a life left is the winner and claims the pool.

PY-RA-MID

1 PLAYER

A game of luck
and arithmetic.
But please,
no calculators!

OBJECT OF THE GAME

To clear away all the cards. The value of a card in your hand plus one uncovered card in the layout must equal 13. Kings are high and Aces are low.

SET UP

DEALER: Shuffle the cards. Lay out 28 cards, face up, in seven rows forming a pyramid. The rows should overlap from bottom to top, as shown.

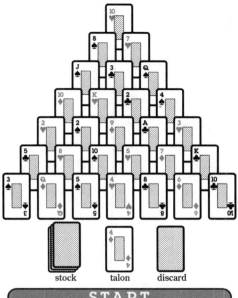

● Put the rest of the deck in a face-down stack in front of you. Turn up the top card. If you add its value to any of the cards on the bottom row, do

the two together equal 13? (A Jack counts for 11, a Queen 12, a King 13, and an Ace 1.)

● If so, pick up both cards and put them face down in a separate discard pile.

● If you can't use the first card to make 13, put it face up next to your face-down stack. This is the start of your "talon" pile.

● Turn over another card from your face-down stack. See if it

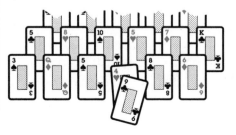

will add up to 13 with any of the available cards. A card is available if it is not covered by another card in the layout.

● You can use the card that you have turned up or the card that is face up on top of the talon pile.

● An available King in the layout or in your hand goes straight to the discard pile.

● The game is over when the face-down stack is gone and all possible combinations of 13 have been made.

● You win the game if you have cleared away the entire layout.

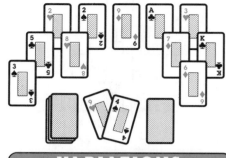

VARIATIONS

● Allow yourself two additional deals when you have run out of plays.

● Allow yourself to make pairs of 13 from the layout.

● Allow yourself to get to 13 using three available cards from the layout.

SEVENS

5, 6, OR 7 PLAYERS

A pretty even split between skill and chance. Also known as Fan Tan, Parliament, and Card Dominoes.

OBJECT OF THE GAME

To play your last card before anyone else. Aces are low (equal to one) in this game.

SET UP

ALL PLAYERS: Pick a card from the deck. Whoever has the highest card deals the first round.

START

DEALER: Shuffle the cards. Deal them all out, one at a time and face down. It's okay if some players have more cards than others.

ALL PLAYERS: Arrange your hand by suit and number—highest cards on the left, lowest cards on the right for each suit.

PLAY

PLAYER ON DEALER'S LEFT: You go first. If you have a Seven, put it on the table, face up. If you can't play a Seven, say "Pass."

NEXT PLAYER: If a Seven has not been played, you must either play one yourself or pass.

● If a Seven has been played, you may play either the Eight or the Six of the same suit.

● Play goes around to the left, with each player adding to the suit if possible, moving up or down in rank. For instance,

STRATEGY

If you have a Six but nothing else in a sequence, keep it in your hand. Your opponents with the Five, Four, Three, Two, and Ace in that suit are stuck.

If you have an Eight, Nine, and Ten in a suit, put out the Eight—your next two turns are guaranteed. Or, don't play the Ten—you'll block the player who's holding the Jack.

Always hang on to your Sevens for as long as you can.

if someone plays an Eight on a Seven, you may play a Six or a Nine.

● If you can't add to the suit, you may start another one by putting out a new Seven next to the first one.

● If you can't add to the suit and don't have any other Sevens, pass.

● The first player to use up all her cards is the winner, but the game continues until all four suits are complete.

ROLLING STONE

4–6 PLAYERS

Cards seem to "roll" from one hand to another. The number of cards you are holding can expand quite suddenly—and so the game is known in France as *Enflé* (inflated), in Germany as *Schwellen* (swollen).

OBJECT OF THE GAME

To get rid of all your cards. Aces are high in this game.

SET UP

ALL PLAYERS: Pick a card from the deck. Whoever has the highest card deals the first round.

DEALER: If you have six players, remove all the Twos from the deck; for five players, remove the Twos, Threes, and Fours; for four players, remove the Twos, Threes, Fours, Fives, and Sixes. Shuffle the cards. Deal them all out, one at a time and face down. Each player should have eight cards.

START

ALL PLAYERS: Arrange your hand by suit—all the cards of

the same suit should be together, with the highest card in each suit on the left, the lowest on the right. Alternate red suits and black suits so that it is easy to see what you have.

PLAYER ON DEALER'S LEFT: You go first. Take a card from your longest (largest) suit and put it face up in the center.

PLAY

● Play goes around to the left. Each player must follow suit (play a card of the same suit).

● If you cannot follow suit, you must pick up all the cards in the middle and add them to your hand.

• Start another round by playing a card from any suit *except* the one just played. For instance, if you were out of diamonds and had to pick up the pile, it will contain a lot of diamonds. But you must then play a heart, spade, or club.

• When everyone has had one turn, the round is over. Put the center pile to one side.

• Whoever played the highest card starts the next round by playing any card he likes from his hand.

• The first player to run out of cards is the winner.

WINNER: Gather up the cards, shuffle them, and deal another game.

I DOUBT IT

4–5 PLAYERS

A great game for risk takers and bluff callers. Also known as Cheat.

OBJECT OF THE GAME

To be the first person to use up all your cards. Aces are low (equal to one) in this game.

I DOUBT IT!

75

SET UP

ALL PLAYERS: Pick a card from the deck. Whoever has the highest card is the dealer for the first round.

DEALER: Shuffle the cards. Deal them all out, one at a time and face down. Don't worry if some players have more cards than others.

START

ALL PLAYERS: Pick up your cards. Sort them by rank (put matching numbers together).

PLAY

PLAYER ON DEALER'S LEFT: You go first. Put out your Aces, face down, in the center.

You can put out all the Aces you have, or you can just pretend to have Aces. Or put out some Aces, plus another card that isn't an Ace—just to see if you can get away with it.

● When you put your cards out, say what they are (or what you're pretending they are)— "Three Aces," for instance.

NEXT PLAYER: Put out whatever Twos you have — or pretend to have.

ALL PLAYERS: Keep taking turns, going around to the left.

Each player must put out the next highest number card. After Kings are played, start again with Aces.

● If you think someone is bluffing (not telling the truth), say "I doubt it."

● If someone doubts you, you must show the cards you played. If you were bluffing, you'll have to pick up all the cards played so far and add them to your hand.

● But if you were telling the truth, all the cards in the center go to the person who doubted you.

● Whoever picks up the pile starts the next round with the next highest number.

● If a player is doubted by two others at exactly the same time, the one sitting closest to the player's left hand is first.

● The first person to get rid of all his cards is the winner.

WINNER: Gather up all the cards and deal the next round.

VARIATIONS

● For a simpler version, each player puts out only one card at a time.

● To make the game shorter, remove the Twos, Threes, Fours, Fives, and Sixes. Remember that Sevens will now follow Aces.

STRATEGY

As in all bluffing games, keeping a straight face is important. Try not to give anything away with moans, groans, or grins.

Remember, it's good for you when someone challenges by mistake. So if you're a good actor, pretend you're bluffing when you're really telling the truth.

As the game nears its end, more people will be bluffing and getting caught—so that's the time to play honest cards if you can.

Try to fill some of the gaps in your hand. If you don't have any low cards, try to challenge the first time low cards are played. If it's early in the game, you'll almost certainly lose your challenge and end up with the low cards you'll need for later on. But don't challenge if the pile in the center is already large.

TRICKS

2–13 PLAYERS

A treat for players ready to move on to "trickier" games. Whist—with training wheels.

OBJECT OF THE GAME

To win the most tricks. Kings are high and Aces are low in this game.

SET UP

ALL PLAYERS: Pick a card from the deck. Whoever has the highest card deals the first game.

DEALER: Shuffle the cards. Deal four cards to each player, one at a time and face down. Put aside the rest of the deck—you won't be using it again for this game.

PLAYER ON DEALER'S LEFT: You go first. Put your highest card face up in the center.

NEXT PLAYER: Put out any card you have of the same suit. If you have two cards of the same suit, put out one that will beat the first player's card,

if possible. You are trying to win the cards in the center— the "trick"—by playing the highest one.

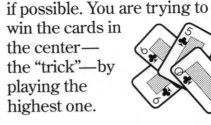

● If you cannot follow suit, put out any other card you like, but try to put out a low card. (You want to save your high cards for later on.)

● Play goes around to the left, with each player trying to follow the suit of the first card played. Otherwise, she plays any other card.

● When everyone has had one turn, stop. Whoever played the highest card in the suit

80

picks up the trick and puts it to one side in a stack.

WINNER OF THE TRICK:
Choose whatever card you like from your hand to start off the next trick. Play the highest card you have—a King, if you can. When everybody has played all their cards, the game is over. Whoever has the most tricks is the winner.

PLAYER ON DEALER'S LEFT:
Gather up all the cards, shuffle them well, and deal another game.

VARIATIONS

● Change the rules a little. Make Aces high, for instance. Then start playing with trumps (see Card Words, page 141). Assign a trump suit each round—spades the first round, hearts the second round, and so on. If someone "leads" trump (plays trump first), then you must play a trump card from your hand. The highest trump card wins the trick.

● When you're used to playing with trump suits, give each player six or seven cards rather than four. Or deal out the whole deck, making sure that everyone has an equal number of cards.

CARDS FOR KIDS

SPIT

2 PLAYERS

A fast-paced, heads-up game. Eye-hand coordination is crucial.

OBJECT OF THE GAME

To get rid of all your cards. Aces are both low and high in this game.

BOTH PLAYERS: Pick a card from the deck. Whoever has the higher card deals.

DEALER: Shuffle the cards. Deal them all out, face down and one at a time. Each player should have a stack of 26 face-down cards.

EACH PLAYER: Lay out ten cards as follows:
Row 1: One card face up, three cards face down.

Row 2: On top of first row, one card face up, two cards face down.

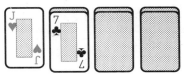

Row 3: On top of second row, one card face up, one card face down.

83

Row 4: On top of third row, one card face up.

Stack the rest of the cards, face down, at the far left of the row. This is your "spit" pile.

PLAY

DEALER: When both of you are ready, shout "Spit!"

EACH PLAYER: Take the top card from your spit pile and put it face up in the center.

● As quickly as possible, play cards in sequence, up or down, from your face-up rows onto either of the center cards.

● If a face-down card is exposed in your layout, turn it face up.

● When both of you are "stopped"—you can't play any

more cards—shout "Spit!" again and put another card from the spit pile into the center.

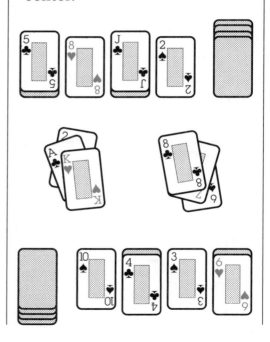

● If neither of you can play any cards onto the cards just played, shout "Spit" again and put out another card.

● If your spit pile runs out, take your pile from the center (leaving the top card), turn it over, and continue playing.

● Shout "Out!" when you have played all the cards from your face-up row. You have won the round.

LOSER: Add your spit pile to the cards from the two piles in the center and the cards left in your face-up row. Shuffle them well.

BOTH PLAYERS: Lay out another ten cards in the same pattern.

● Play as before, but this time if you run out of cards in your spit pile, play without it, borrowing spit cards as needed from your opponent.

● The first player to get rid of all her cards is the winner.

COM-MERCE

3–10 PLAYERS

Get your knuckles in shape for some "knock, knock" fun. Before Poker was invented, thrill seekers got their kicks from Commerce.

86

OBJECT OF THE GAME

To win the most counters by getting as close as possible to one of the three special Commerce hands. Aces are high in this game.

SET UP

● You will need counters — pennies, paper clips, or building blocks, for example. Give

each player the same number of counters.

ALL PLAYERS: Pick a card from the deck. Whoever has the highest card deals the first round.

● Each player contributes one counter to the "pool"—a pile of counters that doesn't belong to anyone until the end of the round.

DEALER: Shuffle the cards. Deal three cards, one at a time and face down, to each player. Put another three cards face up in the center. This hand is called the "widow."

START

● You are aiming for the best possible Commerce hand. There are three kinds.
tricon: three cards of the same rank, with three Aces the highest hand, three Twos the lowest hand.

sequence: three cards in the same suit, in rank order, with Ace-King-Queen the highest, Three-Two-One the lowest.

point: The value of two or three cards of the same suit. Aces equal 11 points, face cards 10 points, other cards face value.

DEALER: You may exchange your entire hand for the widow before play begins.

PLAY

PLAYER ON DEALER'S RIGHT: You're next. You may exchange one card from your hand for a card in the widow.

● Keep going around the table to the right. Players take turns exchanging cards with the widow, trying to make one of the three Commerce hands.

● When you are satisfied with your hand, knock on the table and stop playing.

● When two players have knocked on the table, the game stops.

ALL PLAYERS: Show your hands. Tricon beats sequence. Sequence beats point. A high tricon beats a low tricon. A high sequence beats a low sequence. A three-card point beats a two-card point. If all else is equal, the player nearest the dealer's right hand wins. The dealer always wins a tie.

WINNER: Take the pool.

PLAYER ON DEALER'S RIGHT: Shuffle the cards and deal the next round.

● The person with the most counters after an agreed-upon number of rounds have been played is the winner.

VARIATIONS

TRADE OR BARTER: Do not deal a widow. You may either trade or barter. To trade, you give the dealer a counter and a face-up card, the dealer gives you a face-down card from the deck; then it's someone else's turn. To barter, you offer a card to the player on your right, who accepts or refuses without seeing the card. If you refuse a barter, you "knock" to show you are satisfied with your hand, and the game stops. Best hand wins the pool.

BLACK-JACK

4–6 PLAYERS

Known as Twenty-one at casinos— but just as much fun without the betting. The dealer does most of the work in this game.

OBJECT OF THE GAME

To have a higher point count in your hand—without going over 21—than the dealer.

SET UP

ALL PLAYERS: Pick a card from the deck. Whoever has the highest card deals the first five rounds.

DEALER: Shuffle the cards. Deal one card, face down, to each player, dealing one for yourself last.

● Deal another card, this time face up, to each player including yourself.

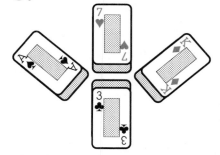

● Look at your face-down card. If the two cards add up to exactly 21, you have a "natural" and automatically win the round, getting one point from each of the other players.

● If you don't have a natural, let everyone else look at their cards without picking them up. Then ask each player in turn, starting on your left, "Will you stand or hit?"

PLAYER ON DEALER'S LEFT: You must decide whether you want another card or not.

● You want your cards to come as close as possible to adding up to 21—without going over. Face cards count as ten, Aces count as either one or eleven; you decide. Other cards get face value.

- If you have a natural, turn over your cards—you automatically win the round and get a point from each player.

- If you are near to 21, say "stand." That means you don't want another card. Keep your face-down card turned down.

- If your cards don't add up to very much or if you have an Ace and can go either way, say "Hit me." That means you want another card.

DEALER: Once you've given a player another card, ask again, "Stand or hit?" A player can have as many additional cards as he wants; all are dealt face up.

ALL PLAYERS: If your cards go over the 21-point limit, you must turn over the cards and say "Bust." You're out of the round.

DEALER: Go once around the table until everyone has had a turn. You go last. Turn over your own cards so that the other players can see them. Then either deal yourself additional hits or stand, as you choose.

- When the dealer is finished, everyone still in the game

STRATEGY

As the dealer, you have all the advantages. Stand if you can.

When you're not the dealer, stand if you have 17 or more points. Less than 11 or 12 points and you'll want to be hit. From 12 to 15 points you're in between; if you get hit, you have a 30% chance of going bust. But if you stand, you'll probably get beat by the dealer.

shows his cards. If you hit 21 exactly, subtract one point from everyone else's score. If someone hasn't scored yet, give him a minus 1. If you stood below 21, mark down one point to anyone who got closer to 21, give yourself one point for each player whose total is less than yours.

DEALER: Pick up the cards and deal another round. After you've dealt five rounds, the deal passes to the player on your left.

● After everyone has dealt five rounds, the person with the most points wins.

CRAZY EIGHTS

2–4 PLAYERS

Fasten your seat belts! Crazy Eights—a.k.a. Switch, Eights, or Swedish Rummy—is a roller coaster ride of card-playing highs and lows. One minute you're on top of the world; one bad play later, you're right back at the bottom. A near-perfect blend of luck and skill.

94

OBJECT OF THE GAME

To get rid of all your cards. Eights are "wild" in this game.

SET UP

● Agree on a winning score—say, 500 points. Set up a score sheet.

ALL PLAYERS: Pick a card from the deck. Whoever has the highest card deals the first round.

START

DEALER: Shuffle the cards. Deal out seven cards to each player, one at a time and face down.

● Place the rest of the deck, face down, in the middle of the table. This is the stock. Turn over the top card from the stock and place it face up alongside. This is known as the "starter."

● If the starter is an Eight, bury it in the stock and turn over the next card.

ALL PLAYERS: Arrange your cards by suit and rank.

PLAY

PLAYER ON DEALER'S LEFT: You go first. Play a card that is either the same suit or the same rank as the starter. For instance, if the starter is the 6♣, you may play any Club or another Six.

● If you can't follow suit or rank, you may play any Eight. Since Eights are wild they can stand for any suit you like, but you must name a suit as you play one.

- If you can't follow suit or rank, and don't have an Eight, take cards from the stock, one at a time, and add them to your hand until you draw a card you can play.

- If the stock runs out before you find a card to play, you must pass.

- Play goes around to the left, with each player trying to match the last card played or pass. The first person to get rid of all his cards wins the round.

LOSERS: Show the winner the cards you have left in your hand. The winner scores 50 points for any Eights you have, 10 points for any face cards or Aces, and face value for all other cards.

- If no one can make any more plays, end the round. The player with the lowest point total in his hand wins. To score the round, subtract the number of points in the winner's hand from the number of points in the other players' hands.

WINNER OF THE ROUND: Gather up the cards, shuffle them well, and deal the next round.

- The first person to reach the point total wins the game.

STRATEGY

Save your Eights for later in the game. If you can't follow suit, you don't have to play an Eight. Pick from the stock instead.

An Eight saved to the very end comes in handy. Play the Eight and name a suit you know has been played out.

Don't give up just because you have more cards than your opponent. If you pay attention and know what's in his hand, you can get rid of quite a few of your cards while he gets rid of none.

VARIATIONS

● For a more skillful game, a player may choose to draw a card from the stock instead of playing a card from his hand.

QUANGO: Aces are wild. If you play a Jack or an Eight, you have another turn. If you play a Seven, the next player must also play a Seven. If she can't, she must pick two cards from the stock. If she can, the next player must also play either a Seven or pick cards from the stock.

KLON-DIKE

1 PLAYER

There are many kinds of Solitaires (one-handed card games), and they have wonderful names like Beleagured Castle, Miss Milligan, Demon, Sultan, and Spider. Klondike is the most common and most popular—as well as the most difficult to win.

OBJECT OF THE GAME

To get all the cards from your hand and from the layout into four piles, one for each suit, with the Ace on the bottom and the King on top.

SET UP

● Shuffle the cards well.

● Deal out 28 cards as follows: Lay out a row of seven cards from left to right, the first card face up, the other six face down.

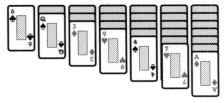

● Skipping the first card, lay out a row of six cards on top of the first; the first card face up, the other five cards face down.

● Skipping the first two cards, lay out a row of five cards, the first card face up, the other

four face down. Continue this way for rows 4 through 7, until you have seven cards in the far right pile, with a face-up card on each pile.

● Put the rest of the deck down in front of you. It is the stock.

START

● Put any Aces which are face up out in front of the layout. These will begin the four foundation piles.

● Turn over the cards underneath any Aces you moved. Put out any Twos you find onto the Aces of the same suit.

● Move cards around on the

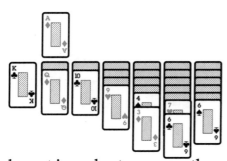

layout in order to expose the face-down cards underneath them. The card you move must be the next rank down from the card you are putting it on, and the opposite color.

PLAY

● When you have made all the plays you can, deal three cards from the stock face down and turn this pile face up on the table.

● If the top card can be played onto the layout or the foundation piles, play it. You can then play the card underneath it.

● If you cannot make a play with the top card, deal three more cards from the stock and turn them face up in the same way, once again looking to see if you can use the top card.

● You may move columns of cards within the layout.

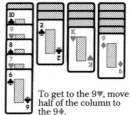

To get to the 9♥, move half of the column to the 9♦.

● You can move parts of columns around to get to a card you want to play.

● You can also play cards from the bottom of a column.

● Kings can be moved to the blank space left when an entire column has been played to the

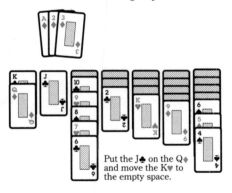

Put the J♣ on the Q♦ and move the K♥ to the empty space.

foundation piles, or cleared.

● You can go through the stock as often as you like, three cards at a time.

● When all the cards are out on the foundation piles, each topped with the appropriate King, you have won the game.

● Gather up the cards, shuffle them *extremely* well, and deal yourself another hand.

CHEATING

● When you get to the point where you can't make any more plays—which often happens in Klondike—you may wish to cheat. If you accept the fact that strictly speaking you've lost the round, you can use the following techniques to get play going again.

● Go through the stock one card at a time instead of three

cards at a time.

● Make a rule that when you get down to six cards in the stock, you can play any of the six cards.

● If you're desperate, just search through the face-down piles until you find the crucial Two, play it, and then carry on as before.

● Just remember, you *have* cheated.

STRATEGY

The most important task in Klondike is to get the face-down cards exposed. So sometimes a card that could be played onto a foundation pile will be more useful as a building card within the layout.

COMET

2 OR MORE PLAYERS

Said to have been invented in France at the time of Halley's Comet in 1759. Also known as Commit. Related to Michigan (Newmarket), Pope Joan, and other games in the Stops family.

OBJECT OF THE GAME

To be the first person to get rid of all your cards. Aces are low in this game.

SET UP

● Remove the 8♦ and as many other Sevens and Eights

 as are necessary to give everyone an equal number of cards.

● Decide what the winning score will be — say, 100 points. Set up a score sheet.

ALL PLAYERS: Pick a card from the deck. The player with the highest card is the dealer for the first round.

START

DEALER: Shuffle the cards. Deal them all out, face down and one at a time.

ALL PLAYERS: Arrange your cards by suit and rank—the highest card in each suit on the left, and the lowest card on the right.

PLAY

PLAYER ON DEALER'S LEFT: You go first. Play the lowest card you have of any suit face up into the center. Announce what the card is as you play it.

● Continue putting out and announcing any cards you have in the sequence and the same suit. For instance, if you put out the 3♥ and also have the 4♥ in your hand, you must play it. When you've played all the possible cards in your hand, your turn is over.

● Play goes around to the left, with each player trying to follow the sequence.

● If you cannot put out the next card in the sequence, say "Without the Eight," "Without the Nine," or "without" whatever you're missing.

● If play goes around the table without anyone being able to make a play, then you have reached a "stop." The player who put down the last card starts a new sequence by putting out the lowest card he has of any suit.

● Kings are natural stops because, as the highest cards in a suit, they end a sequence.

● If you play the King to end a sequence, award yourself one point, then play any other card to start a new sequence.

● The 9♦ is known as the comet. If you have the comet, you may play it any time you like, although you must play it either when the game is stopped or when you cannot continue with a sequence yourself.

PLAYER TO LEFT OF COMET HOLDER: When the comet is

played, you may play either the 10♦ or the next card in the sequence before the comet was played.

● If you can do neither, play passes around to the left until someone can continue.

● The first person to play his final card is the winner and gets one point for every card remaining in the hands of the other players, plus an extra two points for every unplayed King. The player with the comet gets two points — unless he *failed* to play the comet, in which case he must give everyone else one point.

WINNER OF THE ROUND: Gather up the cards, shuffle, and deal another round.

● The first person to reach the point total wins the game.

KNOCK-OUT WHIST

2–7 PLAYERS

This version of Whist is a favorite with those who love tricks-and-trumps games.

OBJECT OF THE GAME

To win the greatest number of tricks and to avoid being knocked out of the game. Aces are high; Twos are low.

107

SET UP

ALL PLAYERS: Pick a card from the deck. Whoever has the highest card deals.

START

DEALER: Shuffle the cards. Deal seven cards, face down and one at a time, to each player. Put the rest of the deck face down in the center.

●Turn over the top card of the stack. That card's suit will be the trump suit for the hand.

Remember: A trump card always beats cards from other suits, but you can't play trump unless you are completely out of the suit that was led (played first).

●Arrange your cards by suit and rank—highest cards to the far left and lowest to the far right in each suit. Alternate

black and red suits.

PLAY

PLAYER ON DEALER'S LEFT: You lead. Put out one card face up in the center. Choose a card from a suit you have lots of, or from a suit you have only one or two of. Avoid playing a high card unless it's an Ace.

NEXT PLAYER: You must follow suit (play another card in the same suit). Try to put out a higher card than the first card.

●If you cannot follow suit,

then either play a trump card or throw away a low card from another suit.

● Play goes around to the left, with everyone playing one card. Whoever played the highest card in the suit or the highest trump card, if any have been played, wins the trick.

WINNER OF THE TRICK: Gather up the cards and put them to one side. Play another card from your hand to start the next trick.

● When all seven tricks have been made, the round is over.

If someone has won all seven tricks the game is over. If you have not taken a single trick, you must drop out.

● Whoever won the most tricks gathers up all the cards, including the stack in the center, shuffles, then deals the next round. This time, only six cards are dealt to each player. In the next round, only five cards are dealt, and so on until in the final round you will each have only one card. Whoever wins this trick wins the game.

● If you win all the tricks in any round, the game is over.

LINGER LONGER

4–6 PLAYERS

An excellent trumps game, where staying power is vital. The tortoise just might beat the hare!

OBJECT OF THE GAME

To be the last player left holding cards. Aces are high in this game.

TICK TOCK
TICK TOCK

Zzzzzz

SET UP

ALL PLAYERS: Pick a card from the deck. Whoever has the highest card deals the first game.

START

DEALER: Shuffle the cards. Deal each player the same number of cards as there are players, giving them out one at a time and face down. Put the rest of the cards in a stack, face down in the middle of the table. This is the stock.

● Turn over the last card you dealt yourself and show it to the other players—its suit is the trump suit for the game. Put the card back in your hand.

● Arrange your cards by suit and rank—highest cards to the far left in each suit, lowest to the far right. Alternate black and red suits.

PLAY

PLAYER ON DEALER'S LEFT: You go first. Play a card face up into the center.

NEXT PLAYER: Either follow

suit or play a trump card. You are trying to win the trick, so play a high card if you can.

● Play goes around to the left until everyone has played a card.

● Whoever played the highest card, or the highest trump card if trump was played, wins the trick.

● Put the cards from the finished trick to one side.

WINNER OF THE TRICK: Take one card from the stock and add it to your hand.

● Start another trick by playing any card you like

from your hand.

● If you run out of cards in your hand, you must drop out of the game.

● The last person to have cards left is the winner.

CARDS FOR KIDS

CATCH
• THE •
TEN

4–6 PLAYERS

In spite of its name, the Jack is the most valuable card in this game. And even though it's sometimes called Scotch Whist, it isn't Whist and doesn't come from Scotland!

OBJECT OF THE GAME

To win the most tricks, especially tricks containing high-scoring trump cards. Aces are high and Sixes are low, except for the trump suit.

SET UP

● Find a pencil and a sheet of paper for keeping score.

● Remove all the Twos, Threes, Fours, and Fives from the deck. If you have five or more players, remove one of the Sixes as well.

ALL PLAYERS: Pick a card from the deck. Whoever has the highest card deals the first round.

START

DEALER: Shuffle the cards. Deal them all out, one at a time and face down. If there are four players, give each player nine cards; if there are five players, give each one seven cards; for six players, give each one six cards.

● Turn up the last card dealt. That card's suit will be the trump suit for the hand. Return the card to your hand.

● In this game, the Jack is the highest card in the trump suit, followed by the Ace, King, Queen, and Ten. But the Ten is worth more points than the face cards, except the Jack.

Remember: You can only play a trump card when you are unable to play a card from the suit that was led (played first).

● Arrange your cards according to suit and rank, highest cards to the left and lowest to the right. Alternate red and black suits.

PLAY

PLAYER ON DEALER'S LEFT: You lead. Put down a card in the center.

NEXT PLAYER: You must follow suit. If you cannot, then play trump or a card from another suit.

● Play goes around to the left until each of you has played a card.

● Whoever played the highest card or the highest trump card, if trump has been played, wins the trick.

WINNER OF THE TRICK: Pick up your trick and put it in a stack to one side.

● Start the next trick by playing any card you like from your hand.

● When all the cards have been played, the round is finished.

ALL PLAYERS: Count up the number of points in the tricks you won: If you won more cards than you had at the start, give yourself one point for each extra card. If you took the following trump cards, you

115

get extra points:

J — 11 points   K — 3 points

10 — 10 points   Q — 2 points

A — 4 points

PLAYER ON DEALER'S LEFT:
Gather up the cards, shuffle, and deal the next round.

● The first player to get 41 points wins the game.

STRATEGY

If you have only one card in a suit, play it early—that way you're void (out of a suit) and can play trump.

If you have the Ace or King of trump, try not to play it until you can use it to capture the much more valuable Ten.

Protect your Ten if you can. If you have lots of low trump cards, keep playing those when others are playing high trump cards. Then play your Ten when you know it will win the trick.

There's nothing you can do about the Jack—it will always go to the player who was dealt it.

GOPS

2 PLAYERS

A bluffer's paradise. Fast and demanding. Perfect for the extra ten minutes before dinner.

OBJECT OF THE GAME

To win as many points in diamonds as possible. Aces are low and Kings are high.

SET UP

● Remove all the hearts from the deck.

● One of you takes all the clubs, the other takes all the spades.

● Shuffle the diamonds and put them in a face-down stack in the center.

START

● Turn over the top
card from the dia-
mond stack.

EACH PLAYER:
Choose a card
and place it face
down in front
of you.

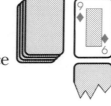

PLAY

EACH PLAYER: Turn up your
face-down card. Whoever has
the higher card wins the diamond.

WINNER OF THE DIAMOND:
Take the diamond card and
put it face up on your right.

EACH PLAYER:
Put the card you
played face up
on your
left.

● Turn up
another
card from
the dia-
mond
stack and
put out another face-down
card.

● If the turned-up cards have
the same rank, turn up another diamond and put out another card from your hand.
Repeat this pattern until the tie
is broken. The highest card
takes the turned-up diamonds.

118

- Continue playing until all the diamonds have been won.

- Add up the diamond points you have won. The Ace is worth 1 point, the other cards face value, the Jack 11, the Queen 12, the King 13.

- The player with the most points wins.

STRATEGY

Keep track of what's been played. This is easy because you know exactly what your opponent started out with.

Watch what she plays and figure out what she has left in her hand. Once she's played her King, she can't beat yours.

Don't play your King to win the A♦ —it's worth only one point. Use your King to win much more valuable cards.

The 8♦, 9♦, and 10♦ can add plenty to your score, so let the other player take the Q♦ and K♦ with his high cards, and then use yours to get the 8♦, 9♦, and 10♦.

KNAVES

3 PLAYERS

Knave is another word for Jack. It also means rogue — for the sort of person who does well in this game.

120

OBJECT OF THE GAME

To win as many tricks as possible without taking any Jacks. Aces are high, Twos are low in this game.

SET UP

● Find a sheet of paper and a pencil for keeping score.

ALL PLAYERS: Pick a card from the deck. Whoever has the highest card deals the first hand.

● Decide how many points a game will be —20 is a good number. You will *lose* points for taking Jacks:

J♥ -4 points
J♦ -3 points
J♠ -2 points
J♣ -1 point

START

DEALER: Shuffle the cards. Deal 17 cards to each player, one at a time and face down.

● Turn up the last card and put it to one side. That card's

suit will be the trump suit for the hand. If the card is a Jack, play the hand without a trump suit (play "no trump").

Remember: Trump beats all other cards, but you can't play trump unless you're "void" in (out of) the suit that was led.

PLAY

PLAYER ON DEALER'S LEFT: You lead. Play any card you like from your hand.

OTHER PLAYERS: Follow suit if you can. Otherwise play trump or a card from another suit.

● Whoever played the highest

STRATEGY

There's no rule against ganging up on a player who's far in the lead. By forming a partnership, two of you can make sure that you get the tricks while the leader gets the Jacks. This means not dumping your Jacks on your new-found friend, even if presented with a golden opportunity. Wait for the leader to play a high card and dump the Jack on him. Your partner does the same. Don't trump your partner's high cards if you can help it; he returns the favor. As soon as the score has evened out a bit, the partnership is dissolved and it's back to everyone for himself!

Lead from your longest suit. Play an unimportant card from the suit you have most of. That way you're not giving away any information about what's in your hand, and you're not hurting your high cards' chances.

Lead a singleton (the only card of a suit) if you

have one. Then you are void in that suit and ready to trump the unsuspecting player who leads it again. Don't play the Ace, King, or Queen of a suit until the Jack has been played or unless you're the last player on the trick.

card, or the highest trump card if trump was played, wins the trick.

●**WINNER OF THE TRICK:**
Pick up the cards and put them face down beside you. Play any card you like to start the next trick. When all the cards have been played, the deal is over.

●**EACH PLAYER:** Give your-

self 1 point for each trick you have taken, minus the points for any Jacks. But if you have taken all four Jacks, add a 10-point bonus.

PLAYER ON DEALER'S LEFT:
Gather up the cards, shuffle them, and deal another hand.

●The first player to get 20 points—or however many you decided on—wins the game.

RUMMY

4–6 PLAYERS

Rummy evolved from Rum Poker, a 19th-century saloon game. The modern version is one of the most popular and widely played card games in the USA.

OBJECT OF THE GAME

To be the first person to get rid of all your cards by collecting cards in certain patterns called "melds." Aces are low and Kings are high in this game.

SET UP

● Find a pencil and a sheet of paper for keeping score.

- Agree on a winning score—50 or 100 points.

ALL PLAYERS: Pick a card from the deck. Whoever has the highest card is the dealer for the first round.

START

DEALER: Shuffle the cards. Ask the player on your right to cut the cards.

- Deal out the cards, one at a time and face down. If there are four players, give each seven cards; for five or six players, deal six cards to each.

- Put the rest of the cards face down in the middle of the table. This is the stock.

- Turn over the top card and put it face up next to the stock. This is the discard pile.

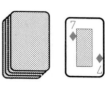

PLAY

PLAYER ON DEALER'S LEFT: You go first. You may pick up the top card from either the discard pile or the stock. Put the card in your hand.

125

- If you have any melds, put them face up on the table in front of you. A meld is either three or four cards of the same rank or three or four cards of the same suit in sequence (number order).

● Discard one card, face up, from your hand to the top of the discard pile. It must not be the same card you picked up.

● Play goes around to the left. Each player takes a turn picking up a card, making melds, and discarding.

● Once other players have put out melds, you may begin "laying off" cards—putting out single cards you have that complete or add on to their melds. For instance, if someone has played three Kings, and you have the fourth King, you may put out your King when it's your turn. Or if someone has put out a meld of the 5♦, 6♦, and 7♦, you may play the 4♦ and 8♦. You cannot add on to someone else's layoff.

● If the stock has run out and you do not want the top card on the discard pile, take the top card off to start a new discard pile and turn over the rest of the cards for a new stock.

● The first player to "go out" (play all his cards) is the winner.

WINNER: Add up the value of the "deadwood" (all the cards left in the other players' hands).

Aces are worth 1 point, other cards get face value, and face cards are 10 points each. The total is your score.

● If you "go rummy"—that is, put out all your melds in one turn (including a discard if you need one), without having

played any melds or laid off on any previous turn—you score double the value of each of your opponent's hands.

PLAYER ON DEALER'S LEFT:

Gather up the cards, shuffle them *extremely* well, and deal out the next hand.

● The first player to reach the agreed-upon score wins the game.

VARIATIONS

ROUND-THE-CORNER RUMMY: Also called High-Low Rummy. Sequences may turn the corner—King-Ace-Two, for instance. An Ace always counts as 11 points, whether used high or low.

QUEEN CITY: Also called One-Meld Rummy. You may go out only by going rummy, with or without a discard. Score the total value of your winning melds, not the dead-wood value of your opponents' hands.

CALL RUMMY: If you see a player discard a card that could have been laid off, you may call "Rummy!" then lay off the card yourself, and replace it with a discard from your own hand. If two call "Rummy!" at the same time, the card goes to the player closest to having another turn.

DISCARD RUMMY: You may go out only if you can end your turn with a discard. You may not play your last card by melding or laying it off.

BLOCK RUMMY: The game

STRATEGY

Watch what the person on your left is doing—don't discard cards he might find useful.

Watch what the person on your right is doing—you are dependent on his discards and will have to shape your melds on what he throws away.

Watch what's going on—what cards other players are picking up from the discard pile, what melds are being put down.

If you are desperate for

MORE STRATEGY

a Seven to put between a Six and an Eight, and you see another player gleefully snap up a Seven from the discard pile, give up. Chances are that player is working on a meld of Sevens; he may, in fact, already have the one you are looking for.

Be flexible. The successful rummy player looks at her hand as potential melds that are changing all the time. Be prepared to move cards from sequence melds to rank melds and back again.

As it's played, each Rummy hand begins to develop a tendency toward either sequence or rank melds. If the other players are putting out rank melds, shift your hand into sequences

Remember that the real penalties come from high cards that get caught as deadwood. So unload a King-and-Jack duo if the Queen hasn't appeared in a short time.

ends as soon as the stock runs out and no one wants the top discard.

BOATHOUSE RUMMY: If you draw the top discard, you must also draw from the stock. Discard one card only. Melds may be made "round the corner." Aces count 11. You cannot meld until one player goes rummy, then everyone else melds what they can. Cards cannot be laid off. Score in the usual way.

KNOCK RUMMY: a.k.a. Poker Rummy. Six cards are dealt to each player. Nothing is melded during play. If you feel you will have less deadwood than other players, knock on the table when it's your turn. Then make all the melds you can, discard one card, and show your deadwood. Other players make all the melds they can. There is no laying off. If you knocked and have the lowest deadwood count, you get as your score the difference between the value of your deadwood and that of each of your opponent's, in turn. You get 25 extra points from each opponent if you went rummy. If you knocked but tie with another player, the other player wins; if someone else has the lowest count, she wins and gets 10 extra points from you.

HEARTS

3–4 PLAYERS

The classic defensive card game. This version, known as Black Lady, Black Maria, or Black Widow, is easily the best.

OBJECT OF THE GAME

To have the lowest score by not taking any hearts or the Q♠ in tricks. Aces are high.

SET UP

● Find a pencil and sheet of paper for keeping score.

131

● If there are only three players, remove the 2♣ from the deck.

ALL PLAYERS: Pick a card from the deck. Whoever has the highest card deals the first hand.

132

START

DEALER: Shuffle the cards. Deal them all out one at a time and face down. If there are three players, you should each have 17 cards; if four, 13 cards.

EACH PLAYER: Arrange your hand by suit and rank, highest card in each suit to the left, lowest card to the right.

● Select three cards from your hand that you don't want, and pass them face down to the player on your right.

● Pick up and put into your hand the three cards passed to you from the left.

PLAY

PLAYER ON DEALER'S LEFT: You lead. Play any card, face up, into the center.

● You cannot lead a heart until hearts have been "broken"— that is, a heart has been discarded by someone who is void in the suit that was led. The Q♠ cannot be discarded on the first trick.

NEXT PLAYER:
You must follow
suit. If you can-
not, you may
either discard a
heart or another
card you don't want.

Remember: Hearts count
against you if you win the
trick.

● Play goes around to the left
until each of you has played a
card.

● Whoever played the highest
card in the suit wins the trick.

WINNER OF THE TRICK: Pick
up the trick and put it face
down in a pile beside you.

● Start the next trick by playing any card you like —
including hearts if they've been
broken — into the center.

● When all the cards have
been played, the round is finished.

● Turn over your tricks and
count up your hearts. Each
heart is worth 1 point against
you; the Q♠ is 13 points
against you. (You may earn a
score of -25 points!)

● But, if you capture all the
hearts *and* the Q♠, you win 26
points — this is called "shooting the moon."

PLAYER ON DEALER'S LEFT:
Gather up the cards, shuffle

them well, and deal the next
round.

● When one player has
reached 50 points, the game
is over. The player with the
lowest score wins. To break a
tie, deal another hand.

VARIATIONS

134

● Try alternating the pass —
to the right on one round, to
the left on the next, across
if there are four players, and
finally no pass.

● Count the J♦ as minus 10
points if you capture it.

● If there are four players,
whoever has the 2♣ leads.

STRATEGY

Will you try to shoot
the moon? If not, you'll
want to get rid of your
high cards; if so, you'll
want to keep them. The
risk is great—if you lose
just one heart and fail to
shoot the moon, you will
be set back by a serious
number of points.

Sometimes shooting
the moon happens by
mistake, but it happens
mostly by design. If you
have a very powerful
hand with lots of high
cards, or lots of cards of

the same suit, it's almost irresistible. But once the other players catch on, they will try to stop you, so you must be able to keep the lead for virtually the entire hand.

It is not always a good idea to pass hearts or the Q♠ to your neighbor. She may then discard the nasties onto a trick you're forced to take. With the Q♠ in your hand, you have more control over where it will end up.

But you don't want to be stuck with it. So, keep your low spades. If you're passed the A♠ or K♠, you can avoid taking the Q♠; if you've got or are passed the Q♠, you won't be forced to play it until you're good and ready—for instance, when someone else plays the K♠.

Pass the A♠ and K♠ unless you're trying to shoot the moon.

Keep your low hearts. They can be distributed evenly to make sure someone else isn't shooting the moon; if hearts have been broken, you can lead low

136

hearts; someone else will have to take them with higher hearts. And if you are passed some high hearts, the low hearts can be played when others are leading hearts, the high hearts dumped when you are void.

If you're not shooting the moon, play your high cards early, before people are void and start dumping hearts. That way you won't be stuck with the lead toward the end of the game, when hearts and the Q♠ are certainly being dumped.

Don't always discard hearts when you're void— this may be the opportunity to get rid of some high cards that are going to get you in trouble later on.

CARD WORDS

A Glossary of Special Terms Used in Card Games

ACE: the first, or number one, card of each suit. An Ace can also be the top card in each suit, above the King. In some games Aces are high (more valuable than Kings), and in some games Aces are low (equal to one).

BLUFF: to pretend to have better— or just different— cards in your hand than you actually hold. In the game I Doubt It, you bluff by lying about the cards you are playing.

BOOK: a collection of four

matching cards. A set of Sevens, for instance, can be called a book. In some games the set is called "four of a kind."

DEADWOOD: in Rummy, the leftover cards in your hand that you weren't able to use in melds by the end of the round. These cards will usually count against you.

DECK: a set of playing cards. A standard deck has 52 cards — 13 cards in each of the four suits. Also called a pack.

DISCARD: to take a card from your hand and put it down either on a discard pile or as part of a trick.

DRAW: to pick a card, usually the top card of a stock or discard pile.

FACE CARDS: the King, Queen, and Jack of each suit. Also called court cards or picture cards. Usually, the Jack ranks above the Ten (or has a value of 11), topped by the Queen (value of 12), then the King (value of 13).

FACE DOWN: with the back of the card showing. The picture or number is down on the table.

FACE UP: with the number or the picture of the card showing. The back of the card is down on the table.

FOLLOW SUIT: to play a card that is the same suit as the lead card in a round or trick, or the same suit as the card played just before your turn.

GAME: a series of deals or rounds, or the target number of points.

GO OUT: to play your last card.

HAND: (1) the cards you were dealt and are holding in your hand, or **(2)** each round of a game, from the time you picked up your cards to when all the cards in your hand have been played.

LAYOUT: the pattern in which you place the cards on the table in Solitaire games. Also called a tableau.

LEAD: to play the first card in a deal, round, or trick.

MELD: in Rummy, the name for the sets of three or four cards that match by rank and/or suit that you are trying to collect. Also, to lay out one or more of these sets.

PAIR: two cards that match rank—two Sevens or two Kings, for instance.

ROUND: a period of play. In some games there is more than one deal. Each time you deal the cards you start a new round.

RANK: (1) the number of a card. For example, the 2♦ and 2♥ are cards of the same rank, or **(2)** the order determining which cards beat other cards.

For instance, Kings usually rank above Queens.

SEQUENCE: a run of cards in order by rank, such as 8, 9, 10, J, Q. In some games, the cards in the sequence must also be of the same suit.

SINGLETON: the one and only card in your hand of a particular suit. Can be very useful in trump games.

STOCK: after the deal, the leftover cards that you are going to use during the game.

SUIT: a set of cards with the same symbol. There are four suits in a standard deck of cards—spades: ♠, hearts: ♥, diamonds: ♦, and clubs: ♣—and there are 13 cards in each suit.

TRICK: the collection of cards, one card played by each player in a round, that is captured by one of the players.

TRUMP: In some games one suit becomes "trump" (is given special power), and is called the trump suit. A card from this suit will beat any card from another suit. For instance, the Two of the trump suit will beat the King of any other suit.

VOID: If you do not have any cards in a particular suit, you are "void" in that suit. Can be very handy in trump games.

WILD CARD: In some games a certain rank is said to be wild. You can pretend a wild card is any card you like, and play it whenever you like.

143